CIVILIZATIONS OF THE WORLD

ANCIENT ROME

by Samantha S. Bell

FOCUS
READERS
NAVIGATOR

WWW.FOCUSREADERS.COM

Focus Readers is distributed by North Star Editions:
sales@northstareditions.com | 888-417-0195

Produced for Focus Readers by Red Line Editorial.

Content Consultant: Joseph McAlhany, Assistant Professor of History, University of Connecticut

Photographs ©: givaga/Shutterstock Images, cover, 1; Songquan Deng/Shutterstock Images, 4–5; Peter Hermes Furian/Shutterstock Images, 7; Vladimir Mucibabic/Shutterstock Images, 8; akg-images/Newscom, 10–11; krivinis/Shutterstock Images, 13; Quintanilla/Shutterstock Images, 15; Oleg Senkov/Shutterstock Images, 16–17; geogphotos/Alamy, 19; Bertl123/Shutterstock Images, 21; Ale Argentieri/Shutterstock Images, 23; Bukhta Yurii/Shutterstock Images, 24–25; Paolo Gallo/Shutterstock Images, 27; Kevin Standage/Shutterstock Images, 28

Library of Congress Cataloging-in-Publication Data
Names: Bell, Samantha, author.
Title: Ancient Rome / by Samantha S. Bell.
Description: Lake Elmo, MN : Focus Readers, 2020. | Series: Civilizations of the world | Includes bibliographical references and index. | Audience: Grades 4-6.
Identifiers: LCCN 2019008551 (print) | LCCN 2019009388 (ebook) | ISBN 9781641859639 (pdf) | ISBN 9781641858946 (ebook) | ISBN 9781641857567 (hardcover) | ISBN 9781641858250 (pbk.)
Subjects: LCSH: Rome--Civilization--Juvenile literature. | Rome--History--Juvenile literature.
Classification: LCC DG77 (ebook) | LCC DG77 .B426 2020 (print) | DDC 937--dc23
LC record available at https://lccn.loc.gov/2019008551

Printed in the United States of America
Mankato, MN
May, 2019

ABOUT THE AUTHOR

Samantha S. Bell lives with her family in South Carolina. She graduated from Furman University with a degree in history and teaching certification in social studies. She is the author of more than 90 nonfiction books for children.

TABLE OF CONTENTS

CHAPTER 1

A VAST EMPIRE

Thousands of people filled the seats of the Colosseum. This huge building was the largest **amphitheater** in ancient Rome. People gathered there to watch **gladiator** fights and other entertainment. The games took place in a flat area at the building's center. Many rows of seats formed a ring around it.

The Colosseum held more than 50,000 people.

Ancient Rome was founded on the Italian peninsula. Rome began as a small village. But over time, the Romans took over a huge area of land. Their **empire** eventually included much of Europe, northern Africa, and the Middle East.

Historians divide ancient Rome into three periods. The regal period lasted from around 753 to 509 BCE. During this time, a series of seven kings ruled Rome. The last king was Tarquin the Proud. After his reign, the Roman Republic began.

During this second period, men from wealthy families took control of the government. Some became members of the Senate. The Senate was a group that advised the rulers. Senators held their positions for life. Romans also elected two consuls each year. The consuls led the Senate. They also commanded Rome's military.

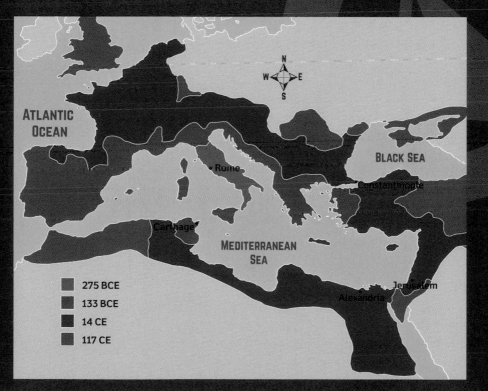

THE ROMAN EMPIRE

ATLANTIC OCEAN

BLACK SEA

Rome

Constantinople

Carthage

MEDITERRANEAN SEA

Jerusalem

Alexandria

- 275 BCE
- 133 BCE
- 14 CE
- 117 CE

Augustus was the first emperor of Rome.

Roman armies won many battles. As Rome grew, its military leaders became more powerful. Some tried to take control of the government. One was Julius Caesar. In 49 BCE, he fought another Roman commander. Caesar won. Afterward, he controlled Rome's government. He even became a **dictator** for life. But his rule did not last long. Senators rose up and killed him in 44 BCE.

In 43 BCE, a group of three men led Rome's government. But they fought one another for total control. The winner was a man named Augustus. By 31 BCE, he had become Rome's first **emperor**. His reign marks the beginning of Imperial Rome. Rome had become a huge empire controlled by one strong ruler.

THE REIGN OF AUGUSTUS

Augustus ruled Rome for 40 years. During this time, he added land throughout Europe and Asia. Rome nearly doubled in size. It also gained more control over the people it ruled. Augustus built many roads throughout the land. He also set up a system of taxes. By his death in 14 CE, Rome was a large and stable empire.

CHAPTER 2

THE PEOPLE OF ROME

Just as Rome's government changed over time, the roles of Rome's people changed as well. In the early Roman Republic, Rome's wealthiest families had the most power. These families were called patricians. They held many political and religious offices, including most of the Senate.

This painting from the 1880s shows what the Roman Senate might have looked like.

Any Roman who was not a patrician was known as a plebeian. Some plebeians did jobs such as farming and building. But others were wealthy. Plebeians also made up much of the Roman army.

For years, plebeians did most of the work while patricians made most of the rules. Around 493 BCE, plebeians demanded more say in government. They refused to work or fight until changes were made.

In response, the patricians created the office of tribune. The tribunes represented the plebeians in Rome's government. The patricians also created assemblies. These groups passed laws

Many important government buildings stood in an area known as the Roman Forum.

and elected leaders. Some even decided punishment for crimes. Any Roman citizen could be part of the assemblies.

Being a Roman citizen was a great privilege. Citizens had many rights that other people in the empire did not. At first, the only ones who could be citizens were people from the city of Rome.

But eventually, conquered people could become citizens, too.

Wealthy Romans often had servants and slaves. Most enslaved people came from outside of Rome. Many were captured during war. But sometimes poor Romans sold their children into

WOMEN IN ROME

Both men and women could be Roman citizens. But female citizens didn't have the same rights. Women could not participate in politics. Instead, they managed the home. Girls usually married when they were young teenagers. Their husbands tended to be much older. Rome had a strict family structure. The oldest living male was the head of each home. He had total control over all other family members.

Stone roads stretched far across the Roman empire.

slavery because they could not care for them. Some people were enslaved for life. Others bought or gained their freedom.

Enslaved people did many different jobs. Some worked in homes or on farms. Others helped build roads and buildings. However, not all enslaved people did hard labor. Some worked as teachers or managed businesses.

CHAPTER 3

DAILY LIFE

Roman emperors had great power over all people. Some emperors even claimed to be part god. The Romans worshipped 12 main gods and goddesses. Jupiter was the king of the gods. He ruled the sky. His brother, Neptune, was god of the sea. Venus was the goddess of love. Mars was the god of war.

Romans often decorated buildings with statues of gods. This statue shows the god Neptune.

The Romans built temples to honor the gods. Priests performed ceremonies and gave offerings. Families also worshipped at shrines in their homes.

Wealthy people often lived near the Roman Forum. This area was at the city's center. It held many temples and government buildings. Wealthy people's

FOUNDING ROME

According to legend, the god Mars had twin sons named Romulus and Remus. When they were babies, a wicked king left them near a river to die. But a wolf found them and raised them. When the boys grew up, they killed the king and planned their own city. But they argued. Romulus killed Remus, so the city of Rome was named after him.

This mosaic shows a man riding a chariot pulled by four horses.

homes had many rooms with beautiful decorations. Romans used colored tiles to create pictures called mosaics. This art covered walls or floors.

Most Roman citizens lived in small apartments with two or three rooms. Apartment buildings were often crowded.

Some buildings were fairly tall, with five or more stories.

Many citizens had to work hard to support their families. They had jobs such as baking, building, or fishing. Even so, Romans found time to relax. Rome's rulers provided free entertainment. People could attend plays and **chariot** races. They could also watch gladiator fights. Some gladiators fought one another with swords, spears, and other weapons. Others battled wild animals, such as lions, elephants, and bears.

Romans also enjoyed the public baths. These huge buildings offered places to read, relax, and talk. They had exercise

The Pont du Gard is a famous Roman aqueduct that still stands in France today.

rooms and swimming pools. To provide enough water for the baths, Romans built aqueducts. These structures used a system of pipes, tunnels, canals, and bridges to bring water into cities. They provided water for fountains, bathrooms, and homes. Aqueducts also carried water across the empire. Some are still used in the city of Rome today.

BUILDING BRIDGES

The Romans were skilled engineers. They built many roads, tunnels, and bridges. Roman bridges could stretch across wide rivers. Some bridges were made from stone blocks. Later, the Romans developed concrete. This material made the bridges stronger and more durable.

The Romans built many arched bridges. This shape helped make the bridges strong. On a flat bridge, the force on the bridge goes straight down. But on an arched bridge, the force goes along the curves to the supports on the end. The arch's curve also helps spread the force evenly through all parts of the bridge. As a result, arched bridges can span longer distances without collapsing.

Hundreds of Roman bridges are still standing. One is the Pons Fabricius. This bridge was built in

The Pons Fabricius connects Tiber Island to land across the Tiber River.

62 BCE. It connects to an island halfway across the Tiber River in Rome. People still use the original bridge.

CHAPTER 4

RULING ROME

Imperial Rome lasted until 476 CE. During this period, many emperors ruled Rome. Not all were good leaders. Nero was one of the most **notorious**. He ruled from 54 to 68 CE. At first, Nero made positive changes, such as lowering taxes. But he later used his power in cruel ways. He had many people killed.

Rome's rulers often stamped their faces on coins as a sign of power.

In 64 CE, a huge fire burned much of Rome. Instead of rebuilding the city, Nero planned a huge new palace. His rule came to an end when soldiers and senators rebelled.

Sometimes the senators elected an emperor because of his abilities. In 98 CE, for example, they chose Trajan. He was a skilled soldier. As emperor, Trajan worked to protect and expand Rome. He fought many battles to gain land. By his death in 117 CE, the empire had reached its largest size.

Hadrian ruled Rome next. Some of Rome's most famous structures were built during his reign. One was the Pantheon.

A hole at the top of the Pantheon's dome lets light into the building.

This building has a huge dome at its center. Another was called Hadrian's Wall. It stretched for 72 miles (117 km) along the edge of Rome's territory in Britain. It was built to keep Rome's enemies out.

Parts of Hadrian's Wall still stand in the United Kingdom.

By 285 CE, Rome faced a variety of problems. Ruling and defending such a huge empire was difficult and expensive. The emperor Diocletian split Rome into two parts. He hoped the smaller areas would be easier to rule.

The western half's emperor lost control in 476 CE. This area split into many pieces. The eastern half became known as the Byzantine Empire. It stayed together longer. But its power faded by 1453. Since then, Rome has had a lasting impact. Many governments are based on ideas from ancient Rome. And buildings often imitate Roman designs.

INFLUENTIAL IDEAS

The Romans adopted many ideas from the Greeks. They even worshipped some of the same gods, though they used different names. During the Roman Republic, a senator named Cicero studied the ideas of Greek **philosophers**. He wrote about their ideas in Latin, the language of Rome. Cicero was also a great speaker. He believed free people should be equal under the law.

FOCUS ON
ANCIENT ROME

Write your answers on a separate piece of paper.

1. Write a letter to a friend describing daily life in ancient Rome.

2. If you lived in ancient Rome, which type of entertainment would you want to try? Why would you choose that one?

3. Who was the first emperor of Rome?
   - **A.** Augustus
   - **B.** Hadrian
   - **C.** Nero

4. How did Hadrian's Wall help protect Rome?
   - **A.** It helped the city of Rome keep animals from escaping.
   - **B.** It helped Romans control who crossed the empire's border.
   - **C.** It kept enemy ships from attacking along the coast of Italy.

Answer key on page 32.

GLOSSARY

amphitheater
A large building with rows of seats that rise around an open space below.

chariot
A two-wheeled vehicle that is pulled by horses.

dictator
A leader with absolute power, especially one who uses that power in a cruel way.

emperor
A powerful ruler who controls a large empire.

empire
A group of nations or territories ruled by a powerful government.

gladiator
A person who fought animals or other people for entertainment in ancient Rome.

notorious
Famous, especially as a result of bad qualities or actions.

philosophers
People who study ideas about truth, knowledge, and the meaning of life.

TO LEARN MORE

BOOKS

Hamen, Susan E. *Ancient Rome*. Minneapolis: Abdo Publishing, 2015.

Nardo, Don. *Daily Life in Ancient Rome*. Chicago: Heinemann Raintree, 2015.

Stokes, Jonathan W. *The Thrifty Guide to Ancient Rome: A Handbook for Time Travelers*. New York: Viking, 2018.

NOTE TO EDUCATORS

Visit **www.focusreaders.com** to find lesson plans, activities, links, and other resources related to this title.

INDEX

Answer Key: 1. Answers will vary; **2.** Answers will vary; **3.** A; **4.** B